INSPIRATIONAL READINGS FOR THOSE WALKING THROUGH CHALLENGES

TRACEY D. GILCHRIST, M.ED.

Book Cover Design: Prize Publishing House
Book Cover Design Inspired By: Sally Jones

Printed by Prize Publishing House, LLC in
the United States of America.

First printing edition 2024.

Prize Publishing House
P.O. Box 9856, Chesapeake, VA 23321
www.PrizePublishingHouse.com

ISBN (Paperback): 979-8-9908345-2-1
ISBN (E-Book): 979-8-9908345-3-8

Contents

Acknowledgments

I am thoroughly convinced that every high and low place in our lives can be purposeful if our focus is shifted and our spiritual ears are attentive to God's voice. Once His utterance is heard, whether audibly or not, obedience and action are the next logical steps. Often, there is a necessary time of preparation and waiting that takes place for various reasons. Sometimes it is because we want to be sure of what we heard and the direction that we are to take next. Other times, we are distracted, and the gift of time gently passes inconspicuously. Regardless, our spirits will not be settled until our feet are actively on our path of purpose. Sometimes, our pace on that path feels like lightning speed, while other times, a snail's pace seems way too fast. Regardless, forward movement is the expectation despite our high and low places in life. It is with this perspective that this work was born. My cancer journey was both my mountain and my valley simultaneously, yet I rose by the power and grace of God! I want to thank all who prayed for and supported me through that ordeal. There are too many to acknowledge here, but please know that your support helped pull me through. You took the time to pray for me, and I am so thankful.

To my husband, Rodney, and my forever babies (Jamie, Rodney Jr, and Jordan), you are my everything! How kind of God to give me you. To my siblings (Michael and Maureen) and their families, how could I have made it without you? Thank you for everything!

I am grateful that my beloved mother, Sally, was able to read every God-inspired word of this work, inspire my cover design through her love of coloring, and write a foreword prior to her transition. God is so loving and kind to allow that. Your legacy lives on in so many who were blessed to love and know you, especially your children and grandchildren. Continue to rest in His presence.

And to my father, Reginald, who transitioned long before this work came to fruition, I honor you. You live on in your children and some of your traits are evident in grandchildren that you never even met. God is so wise. I love you all!

"Arise, shine; for thy light is come, and the glory of the Lord is risen upon thee."
- Isaiah 60:1 (KJV)

Foreword

"As we journey through life, we encounter many situations. There is a purpose for everything that we go through. If we have a heart of God, our desire is to impact others. That is how we reach our brothers and sisters and, thereby, draw others to Christ. It also encourages us to know that whatever we go through, it is all for God's glory. These poems and inspirational readings are from my daughter, Tracey Gilchrist's actual experience. God bless you!"

Message from my mother,
Sally E. Jones (10/22/1945 - 11/10/2023)

"Tracey, when I look at you now versus the beginning of your journey, all I can do is praise God. There were times of uncertainty for me. Will I lose my sister, the best friend I've ever had? I watched sometimes in silence but most times in fear. Then something awakened in me, and I was determined to hold on with all my might. I wanted to make sure I was available for whatever the need was. I cried out to God and proclaimed that I did not know the end, but He did. I was determined to fight for you. I bless God!"

Message from my sister, Maureen Gay

"Tracey, I'm so proud of the woman you have become and happy for your next chapter. God never promised that we would not have trials. However, in Romans 5:3-5 MSG, we are reminded of this: 'There's more to come. We continue to shout our praise even when we're hemmed in with troubles because we know how troubles can develop passionate patience in us and how that patience, in turn, forges the tempered steel of virtue, keeping us alert for whatever God will do next.' God spared you for this moment, the NEXT in your life."

Message from my brother, Michael Drew

An Unusual Peace

Who would have thought that I would be
walking through this rocky terrain?
It was like, out of nowhere, the ground
shifted below my feet.
The thoughts, fears, uncertainty, and changes
seemed to bombard me all at once.
Although the transitions just kept coming one right
after the other, there was still an unusual peace.
An unusual peace that increased my
faith and hope in the future.
An unusual peace that birthed a smile when the
expected response was a somber disposition.
An unusual peace that allowed me to
still anticipate a promising future.
An unusual peace that caused me to focus on
the treatment plan with great anticipation.
An unusual peace.... THAT ONLY GOD CAN GIVE.
That is what I was blessed to experience - an unusual
peace that gave me joy in the middle of this storm.
This storm is a controlled storm because
nothing takes God by surprise.

SCRIPTURE REFERENCES

Psalm 139; John 14:27; Isaiah 26:3; Psalm 4:8

MORNING MEDITATION

_____

_____

_____

_____

_____

_____

_____

_____

_____

_____

_____

_____

_____

_____

_____

_____

EVENING ENCOURAGEMENT

_____

_____

_____

_____

_____

_____

_____

_____

_____

_____

_____

_____

_____

_____

_____

_____

_____

_____

_____

WORDS OF LIFE TO MYSELF

Why Not Me?

I never thought that I'd be in this place, with
this appearance, and with these limitations.
If you'd asked me a few years ago, I would
not have envisioned this current self.
Sometimes the challenges feel overwhelming
and difficult to endure.
I almost begin to feel pity when I look in the mirror
and wonder why I was selected for this trial, but
then I hear deep in my soul…. "Why not me?"
Why me as I look around and see that others
seem to be improving and thriving?
Why me as I see those who appear
like the picture of health?
Then the Holy Spirit speaks peace to my soul
and reminds me that He is here and because
He chose to preserve my life, so am I.
He reminds me that my presence and current
existence are nothing short of a miracle.
He reminds me that there is a purpose behind
this season of transition and change.
He reminds me that I was hand-selected so that I
could grow and know Him like never before.
As I reflect on all the answers to "why
me," I begin to rejoice because I clearly
see the intentionality of my Creator.
Why me? Why not me?!? Thank
You, Lord, for choosing me.

SCRIPTURE REFERENCES

John 15:16; James 1:2-4; 1 Corinthians 10:12-13

MORNING MEDITATION

_____

_____

_____

_____

_____

_____

_____

_____

_____

_____

_____

_____

_____

_____

_____

_____

EVENING ENCOURAGEMENT

WORDS OF LIFE TO MYSELF

Nothing Takes God By Surprise

You have brought me to this place for a purpose, so I
embrace that purpose and I rest in Your sovereignty.
Twists and turns, hills and valleys, joy and
sorrow, but Your peace still comforts me
despite what I see....just knowing.
Nothing takes You by surprise.
It's all working for Your glory.
I'll be Your instrument for the world
to see and embrace peace.
Because nothing takes You by surprise.
My life is in Your hands no matter what lies ahead.
You remain in full control no matter what the world says.
Crises, pandemics, failures, sickness, and
calamity all must bow at your feet.
You reign victoriously! You are my King!
Because nothing takes You by surprise.
It's all working for Your glory.
You're pruning me to what You created
me to be, so I'll go on....
Because nothing takes You by surprise.

SCRIPTURE REFERENCES

Psalm 139; Jeremiah 29:11; Romans 8:28

MORNING MEDITATION

EVENING ENCOURAGEMENT

WORDS OF LIFE TO MYSELF

_____

_____

_____

_____

_____

_____

_____

_____

_____

_____

_____

_____

_____

_____

_____

_____

_____

_____

_____

_____

Sweet Peace

Who ever knew that I'd be at this place?
My plans were different; my goals were set,
I was comfortable in my space.
Then, change came so suddenly.
My world was shaken; my life was altered.
Everything quickly changed for me.
Yet I had sweet peace, the kind
that words can't describe.
God took my hand and renewed my mind again.
Yes, I have sweet peace, the kind
that's hard to understand.
God spoke, "Be still," which helped me to heal.
It's His sweet peace!

SCRIPTURE REFERENCES

Matthew 8:23–27; Mark 4:35–41; Luke 8:22–25

MORNING MEDITATION

_____

_____

_____

_____

_____

_____

_____

_____

_____

_____

_____

_____

_____

_____

_____

_____

EVENING ENCOURAGEMENT

WORDS OF LIFE TO MYSELF

Smile Anyway

So, you say that you can't understand why I smile
when my body seems to be turning on itself?
So, you wonder why my hands go up in praise, even
when it hurts to even lift a finger sometimes?
Are you confused by the joy that breaks forth
on my face when we see one another?
Are you perplexed by the inconsistency between the
reality of the diagnosis and what you actually see?
How shocked are you by the astonishment on the care
team's faces when I smile despite the medical report?
Even I am baffled by the songs that spring forth even
when the physical pain seems more than I can bear.
Yes, I have a melody in my heart, although the impact
of treatments seemed to have stifled my speech.
Why? Because I know that there is a purpose and a plan
for all of this…if not for me, then for someone else.
Because of that…. I smile anyway.

SCRIPTURE REFERENCES

Psalm 32:11; Philippians 4:4; Romans 12:12

MORNING MEDITATION

_____

_____

_____

_____

_____

_____

_____

_____

_____

_____

_____

_____

_____

_____

_____

EVENING ENCOURAGEMENT

WORDS OF LIFE TO MYSELF

Fear Not

Never before have I experienced anything like this.
I don't even recall all the details
of how I got to this point.
I am worried about what's ahead, but I
know that I can't relive my past.
The fluttering in my stomach is an expression
of the uneasiness in my mind.
The hows, whys, and whens just keep replaying
in my mind like a familiar rhythmic melody.
But then, I hear a more melodious sound that
speaks undeniable peace to my very soul.
"Fear not! You are not alone, nor have you ever been."
"Fear Not! I was with you even when
you felt the most alone."
"Fear Not! I always had a plan;
nothing was ever in disarray."
"Fear Not! I am creating in you a fortitude
that only this fire can refine."
"Fear Not! Your story is still being written,
and the ending is going to be more beautiful
than you could ever pen on your own."
"Fear Not! This trial is making a great exchange
within you, and you'll be stronger than ever before."
"Fear Not! The GREAT I AM is here!"

SCRIPTURE REFERENCES

Isaiah 41:10; Isaiah 43:1-13

MORNING MEDITATION

EVENING ENCOURAGEMENT

_____

_____

_____

_____

_____

_____

_____

_____

_____

_____

_____

_____

_____

_____

_____

_____

_____

_____

WORDS OF LIFE TO MYSELF

Live Life

We all long to make our "dash" memorable, impactful, and a legacy for future generations, but what do we do when our "dash" is questioned and even challenged by an unexpected event? Our dash is the timeframe between when we were born and when we passed away. What we do with the "dash" that we are given depends on us. Sometimes, we directly impact the fruitfulness of our "dash," while other times, we have little or no control over the influential factors. Regardless, we are admonished to LIVE! Life happens, challenges come, rain falls, and storms arise. Conversely, the sun shines, flowers bloom, daybreaks happen, and waters cease. See, seasons happen, and each one has an intended purpose. Regardless, we are challenged to speak LIFE. Whatever happens and whatever challenges we face, choose to LIVE LIFE! Receive the purpose that is within each season and dismiss the chaff. As we go through, grow through, and LIVE!

SCRIPTURE REFERENCES

Ecclesiastes 3:1-8; John 10:10; Romans 5:1-11

MORNING MEDITATION

EVENING ENCOURAGEMENT

WORDS OF LIFE TO MYSELF

Press In

Nausea, neuropathy, insomnia, debilitating body
pain, scars, speech slurs, brain fog, instability, lack of
strength, low to no energy, memory loss, no stamina…
BUT…
I PRESS!!
Hope, faith over fear, mountain mover, joy,
compassion, worship, trust, provision, belief,
gradual improvement, growth, motivation…
If the cycle repeats, **I WILL STILL PRESS**!!

SCRIPTURE REFERENCES

Philippians 3:13-14; 1 Timothy 6:11-12; Psalm 34

MORNING MEDITATION

EVENING ENCOURAGEMENT

WORDS OF LIFE TO MYSELF

_____

_____

_____

_____

_____

_____

_____

_____

_____

_____

_____

_____

_____

_____

_____

_____

_____

_____

_____

The Miracle Of My Faith

Worshiping and praising God through storms is critical.
An atmosphere is created that invites God to sit in the
middle of what is going on and exchange tumultuous
waters for peace. Before we realize it, we'll be in a
beautiful place full of love, understanding, and guidance.
Worries and concerns can be confessed
and the heaviness of them lifted.
Praise God for the privilege to worship Him in the
middle of a mess, in the presence of pain, in the weight
of worry, and in the uncertainty of unsettled times.
It is there that an amazing transformation takes
place, and remarkable renewal blooms.
That, within itself, lies the miracle of my faith.

SCRIPTURE REFERENCES

Revelation 21:5; Hebrews 11:1; Psalm 61:1-3

MORNING MEDITATION

EVENING ENCOURAGEMENT

WORDS OF LIFE TO MYSELF

Thank The Thorn

Thorns can be annoying, invasive, prickly, unwanted, and a distraction. But have we ever thought about the blessing of thorns? Sometimes things happen to help redirect our focus and energy towards kingdom principles. We often get on autopilot and feel that we are the captain of our own ships and the master of our own lives. We often feel self-sufficient and independent of divine direction and help in our lives. That mentality is so far from the truth. We breathe God's air, and we walk because of God's strength. We exist only because God allows us to and only for His glory. God wants to use every ounce of our experiences. Nothing will be wasted if we yield it to Him. Even that thing that appears to be a thorn in our lives, God can use it all to bring Him glory and to keep us in a posture of hearing His voice and obeying Him each day. So today, we allow ourselves to thank the thorn that God allows. If He does not allow it to leave, He will allow it to be impactful if only we will let ourselves GROW through while we GO through. Thank the thorn!

SCRIPTURE REFERENCES

2 Corinthians 12:7-10; 1 Corinthians 3:5-7; Romans 12:1-2

MORNING MEDITATION

EVENING ENCOURAGEMENT

WORDS OF LIFE TO MYSELF

_____

_____

_____

_____

_____

_____

_____

_____

_____

_____

_____

_____

_____

_____

_____

_____

_____

_____

_____

_____

He Never Said It Would Be Pretty

Loss of hair and weight…transformation of skin tone….
dark nails…. loss of eyebrows and lashes…. droopy
eyes, and a gaited walk…. grimaces on my face from
joint pain as I walk…but I am beautiful inside.
I am being transformed and changed for God's glory.
He is making me over as I sit on the potter's wheel.
God never said that my delivery process would be
pretty, but it will surely speak a word of deliverance to
those who need it if I remain committed to the journey.
Sometimes the road that leads to deliverance is bumpy.
This only makes the journey relatable and more
of an opportunity for God to be glorified.
The process is not pretty, but it sure is precious
in God's sight if we remain faithful.

SCRIPTURE REFERENCES

Jeremiah 18:1-6; Acts 27:27-44; 2 Samuel 4:1-4; 2 Samuel 9

MORNING MEDITATION

EVENING ENCOURAGEMENT

_____

_____

_____

_____

_____

_____

_____

_____

_____

_____

_____

_____

_____

_____

_____

_____

_____

_____

_____

_____

WORDS OF LIFE TO MYSELF

All Is Well Today

I don't know why my life has taken
these detours and pitstops.
What I see is far from what I expected
for myself and my loved ones.
I didn't wake up realizing that I would hear
this life-altering news throughout the day.
Things happen so quickly, and change
happens with no warning at all.
Even in all of that, I can still say that all is well today.
The one thing that I believe is that the
thing did not come to destroy me.
It only came to make me better and draw
me closer to Your purpose for my life.
Even when I begin to feel emotionally overcome
by my current situation, You open my eyes.
You allow me to see the future, my
legacy, and my testimony.
You help me to see that there is a reason for this test.
Despite what my natural eyes see and my fleshly
heart feels, I know that all is well today.
So, my spiritual response will be a joyful
heart and exuberant praise!
God is in the midst of it all; He has not abandoned me.
He is walking right beside me and carries me
when my legs are too weak to prop me up.
My faith tells me that all is well today, so I
choose to listen and rest in that fact.

SCRIPTURE REFERENCES

Psalm 30; 2 Corinthians 4:17; Psalm 16:11; Isaiah 38:3-5

MORNING MEDITATION

EVENING ENCOURAGEMENT

_____

_____

_____

_____

_____

_____

_____

_____

_____

_____

_____

_____

_____

_____

_____

_____

_____

_____

_____

WORDS OF LIFE TO MYSELF

He Stayed Two More Days

I called Him and I could feel in my spirit that He
heard me, but He stayed two more days.
My body was aching and seemed to become weaker
and more disfigured, but He stayed two more days.
The medical appointments were so numerous that
I had to write them all down, as I couldn't afford to
miss one of them. Yet He stayed two more days.
Peeling skin from radiation and numb fingers and toes
from chemotherapy....yet He stayed two more days.
I could see the concern on the faces of my
family, especially when my body got weaker by
the day.... but He still stayed two more days.
He stayed two more days so that He could
receive all glory. He stayed two more days
so that my faith would increase and my
mountains would know that Jesus is Lord!

You stayed two more days so that all who knew me
and my story would have convincing, indisputable
evidence of Your power and sovereignty.
Thank You for staying two more days!

SCRIPTURE REFERENCES

John 11:1-44

MORNING MEDITATION

_____

_____

_____

_____

_____

_____

_____

_____

_____

_____

_____

_____

_____

_____

_____

_____

_____

EVENING ENCOURAGEMENT

WORDS OF LIFE TO MYSELF

_____

_____

_____

_____

_____

_____

_____

_____

_____

_____

_____

_____

_____

_____

_____

_____

_____

_____

_____

_____

_____

Healing Beyond The Diagnosis

The specialists guided me through what to
expect and the duration of this pain.
The treatment plan was well-
documented and easily accessible.
Medical information is in abundance, which is
both helpful and daunting at the same time.
Too much too soon only made me feel worse sometimes,
but at least I could navigate through the knowledge.
But THIS HURT...far beyond the diagnosis,
was most difficult and heartbreaking.
THIS HURT flew below the public radar, only
seeming to accelerate the growth rate.
THIS HURT caused an emptiness that
no pill or port could cure.
THIS HURT left me emotionally limp and powerless.
All I had was confidence that God sees
and understands, and a reality that my
emptiness was true and not imagined.
I needed to know that God loved me enough to
feel and understand my pain and that in His way
and timing, He would make everything alright.
So, I continue to praise Him in advance
for healing beyond my diagnosis.
I could navigate the diagnosis with God's help, but
only God can mend my heart from...THIS HURT.

SCRIPTURE REFERENCES

Psalm 61; Psalm 147:3; Psalm 73:26

MORNING MEDITATION

_____

_____

_____

_____

_____

_____

_____

_____

_____

_____

_____

_____

_____

_____

_____

EVENING ENCOURAGEMENT

WORDS OF LIFE TO MYSELF

Fullness In My Empty Place

Vivacious, fun, goal-oriented, intrinsically
motivated, high energy....
Those are just a few words that described
me before you invaded my life.
Settled, comfortable, even robotic at times....
That was my routine before you
forced your way into my life.
Although I was occupied, I was not
necessarily full of all that I needed....
Until you stepped into my life so
aggressively that everyone noticed.
You changed me externally but
transformed me internally as well.
I thought I was full and complete, but
emptier than I realized....
Until you stepped into my life and changed
my focus, vision, and motivation.
For that I can only express gratitude and appreciation
for that transformation that came with your visitation.
Although it was my hardest fight, it was
also my most treasured victory.
By God's strength and mercy, my empty places
were made full again, and I am brand new.
I am beyond thankful for the fullness that
overshadowed me in my empty place!

SCRIPTURE REFERENCES

2 Corinthians 12:9-10; Genesis 50:19-21

MORNING MEDITATION

EVENING ENCOURAGEMENT

WORDS OF LIFE TO MYSELF

Because You're With Me

As I consider the road ahead, I'm overcome
with both gratitude and uncertainty.
I know that my future is in God's hands, but
I often wonder what it will look like.
Together my God and I have overcome so much.
You have carried me through storms and
shielded me from destruction.
You have allowed me to rest in green pastures
and also ride the waves of strong seas.
You have renewed my strength and
lifted my hung-down head.
You have caused a smile to return when
circumstances would have caused me to
be discouraged for way too long.
I can move forward because You're with me.
Because You're with me, I have hope.
Because You're with me, I can dream again.
Because You're with me, I can take up my bed and walk.
Because You're with me, I can be brave.
Because You're with me, I can and will rejoice.
I will not be afraid of what lies ahead
because You're with me.

SCRIPTURE REFERENCES

Psalm 23; Isaiah 41:10; Romans 8:31; Psalm 46:7

MORNING MEDITATION

EVENING ENCOURAGEMENT

_____

_____

_____

_____

_____

_____

_____

_____

_____

_____

_____

_____

_____

_____

_____

_____

_____

_____

WORDS OF LIFE TO MYSELF

I've Been Through Too Much Not To Praise God

My heart feels so overwhelmed when I reflect
on all that I've endured recently.
There have been so many hurdles and
trials, yet God's favor is radiating.
I know that there is a purpose in all of this
pain, even if my heart does not feel it.
Our hearts are not always clear on the reality
of God's plan, and how could it be?
It is simply a conglomerate of flesh and emotions
that sometimes gets its signals crossed.
If I think too hard, I just might begin to feel overwhelmed
because of everything that I have walked through lately.
I tell myself that it is healthy to express
where I am emotionally, but I caution myself
about staying in that space too long.
You see, I have been through too much not to praise God.
He has carried me through so many rugged hills and valleys,
not to mention the unknown snares that escaped me.
Yes, I hurt and experience disappointments
far too often than I wish to admit.
Yes, I feel like my life is frozen sometimes because of
the simple desires that are far from my control.
Yes, despondency seems to overtake me
and leave me bewildered.... but yet!
I have been through too much not to praise God,
so I stay close to Him and talk with Him.
I know that He hears me...even those
things that only my spirit speaks.
I will continue to run my race with patience, knowing
that I have been through too much not to praise Him!

SCRIPTURE REFERENCES

Psalm 34; Isaiah 41:10; 1 Thessalonians 5:16-18

MORNING MEDITATION

_____

_____

_____

_____

_____

_____

_____

_____

_____

_____

_____

_____

_____

_____

_____

_____

_____

EVENING ENCOURAGEMENT

WORDS OF LIFE TO MYSELF

_____

_____

_____

_____

_____

_____

_____

_____

_____

_____

_____

_____

_____

_____

_____

_____

_____

_____

_____

_____

The Remaking

Changes in the body, bloodwork,
therapy, new diagnoses....
So much seems to be happening at once
to both me and my loved ones.
Yet there is a peace that is happily overwhelming.
Early this morning, it was revealed just
why that peace was overtaking me....
This process was more of a remaking than a
breaking down. Lord, you are doing something
new and magnificent because the old was
insufficient for the glory that shall be revealed.
It's amazing how we pray and cry out to
God for certain things, but when it actually
comes to pass, it comes as a surprise.
It's time to get intimately acquainted with the new, the
upgrade, the abundance, and the unexplainable joy.
These physical changes that we're experiencing
are in the capable hands of our Savior. Rest in
Him and make way for the REMAKING. It's going
to be like nothing we've ever seen before!

SCRIPTURE REFERENCES

Isaiah 43:19-21; Jeremiah 18:1-10

MORNING MEDITATION

_____

_____

_____

_____

_____

_____

_____

_____

_____

_____

_____

_____

_____

_____

_____

_____

EVENING ENCOURAGEMENT

WORDS OF LIFE TO MYSELF

_____

_____

_____

_____

_____

_____

_____

_____

_____

_____

_____

_____

_____

_____

_____

_____

_____

_____

_____

_____

My Feet Almost Slipped

I can't afford to wallow in the mud of this
test. There are too many giants to slay
and too many testimonies to share.
Since we are overcome by the blood of the Lamb
and the words of our testimony, I know I can't keep
silent. Even through my storms, Lord, help me to
graciously walk through honorably for Your glory.
Stopping here is not an option. If I stop here, how
will my circle know that You're a mighty deliverer
whose power is never diminished by the intensity
of the heat or length of the season of affliction?
With that in mind, I will pursue You with all my might
because I know that this season will yield an abundant
harvest that will extend to many future generations.
This will happen if, and only if, I stay at Your feet
and never quit. Thank You, Lord, for Your comfort
that wraps me up and keeps me warm through the
harsh elements. You are worthy to be praised!

SCRIPTURE REFERENCES

Psalm 73; James 1:12; 2 Corinthians 12:9-10

MORNING MEDITATION

EVENING ENCOURAGEMENT

_____

_____

_____

_____

_____

_____

_____

_____

_____

_____

_____

_____

_____

_____

_____

_____

_____

_____

_____

WORDS OF LIFE TO MYSELF

Walk Through The Doubt

Healing, victory, and deliverance are all my
portion. I know it, I walk it, and I speak it,
but sometimes, I experience doubt.
I am fully convinced that You love me with an
everlasting love, but sometimes I wonder why.
I am so imperfect, and sometimes I
struggle with myself and my ways.
I have doubts sometimes, but I believe You. I trust that
You are for me and that You are allowing all things (and
I do mean ALL things) to work out for my benefit.
Although I have uncertainty, I will walk through
and triumph over my doubts. I will love through my
doubts, I will praise while I doubt, and I will pursue
You through my doubts. I do this because I know
that doubt is simply a byproduct of my humanity
and humility. I will be strong in You alone because
there is inadequate strength in me. But in You, I
have all that I need. And because I do, I can praise
You even if I experience doubt. I will walk through
every trial with Your strength as I pursue Your heart,
and before I realize it, doubt begins to dissipate.

SCRIPTURE REFERENCES

Proverbs 3:5-8; Mark 9:21-24

MORNING MEDITATION

_____

_____

_____

_____

_____

_____

_____

_____

_____

_____

_____

_____

_____

_____

_____

_____

EVENING ENCOURAGEMENT

WORDS OF LIFE TO MYSELF

Indescribable Joy

It is so difficult to explain the peace and joy that
I feel right in the midst of my struggles.
There is so much uncertainty and reasons
to be concerned and overwhelmed.
Yet, I feel peace and reassurance of God's presence
and power right in the middle of my storm.
This joy is simply unexplainable,
unfathomable, indescribable…. there
aren't adequate words to explain it.
I know that there is nothing that I did to earn it;
I could not gift myself with this even if I tried.
But today, I celebrate the indescribable joy
that I feel despite what my eyes see.
I know that peace can only come from God, who
loves and protects me beyond my strength.
I feel so overwhelmed by His compassion for
me and for those whom I love so dearly.
He protects and keeps us in the cocoon of
His care, shielding us from what could have
been…. should have been….may have been if
He had not extended His mercy and grace.
Yes, so much has happened, but I stand in amazement
at all that He kept us from and through.
There are no words to explain this indescribable joy
so I will allow my heart to leap in contentment and
rest peacefully just knowing that God did it again!
He has bestowed indescribable joy!

SCRIPTURE REFERENCES

Philippians 4:4; Psalm 16:11; Habakkuk 3:17-18

MORNING MEDITATION

EVENING ENCOURAGEMENT

WORDS OF LIFE TO MYSELF

Lord, Help Me To See What You See

As we live this life, we observe events that
produce both joy and great sadness.
Often it is difficult to understand it all,
and even more difficult to accept it all, but
Lord, help us to see what You see.
As we strive daily to make a difference in the lives of
others and effect positive change, we often wonder if our
efforts are making a difference. The needs sometimes
seem so great, but Lord, help us to see what You see.
For if we see what You see, then we can understand that
our efforts are just a small part of a much greater plan.
If we see what You see, then our souls will be
quieted when they begin to feel overwhelmed
by all that our hands have been given to do.
If we see what You see, then we can rest in You,
knowing that all things will work out for our
good and for the good of those so dear to us.
If we see what You see, then we will be
reminded that our labor is not in vain.
Lord, in all seasons of life, help us to see what You see.

SCRIPTURE REFERENCES

Psalm 62:5; Luke 10:38-42; Romans 8:28

MORNING MEDITATION

EVENING ENCOURAGEMENT

WORDS OF LIFE TO MYSELF

Built To Last

Cell by cell, bone by bone, molecule by
molecule, emotion by emotion….
God built me in His perfect image
with just one spoken word.
Regardless of my trials and obstacles,
I know I was meant to be here.
Despite my challenges and inability to put all the pieces
together, I am fully convinced that I was built to last.
Often when we endure storms, our vision becomes
cloudy of what God intended us to be.
Sometimes we lose sight of our purpose or the
fact that God allowed these challenges to come
in order for us to be drawn closer to Him.
Then, out of nowhere, a still, small voice
reminds me that I was built to last.
This intense pain is not my end. This debilitating
but temporary suffering is certainly not
where my story will stop being written.
I know that there is purpose behind this pain and
that I will rise from the ashes with more than I had
before the winds of this storm began to howl.
I was built to last, so I will hold fast to the anchor
that keeps me steady despite the winds.

SCRIPTURE REFERENCES

Matthew 7:24-29; Psalm 18:2; Luke 6:47-48

MORNING MEDITATION

EVENING ENCOURAGEMENT

WORDS OF LIFE TO MYSELF

Living Water

Water is powerful and fulfills so many purposes.
It is a cleanser and provides refreshment.
It can be still but can also be tumultuous.
It can be used for leisure but can also
be used for transportation.
It moves objects and people while it also
remains still and anchors objects.
Water is to be admired but also respected.
So, it is with the trials of this life.
Sometimes I need refreshment as I endure various trials.
At times, I only need to be still and
reflect on God's goodness.
I need His strength to carry me through every trial.
I need His peace to quiet my spirit when
I start to feel overwhelmed.
I need His living water to wash over my soul
and restore me in every area of my life.
His presence is the only thing that can satisfy
my soul's longing, so I run to Him.
I chase His presence and the restoration of His living
water. There is satisfaction in no other place.

SCRIPTURE REFERENCES

John 4:1-26; John 7:38-39

MORNING MEDITATION

_____

_____

_____

_____

_____

_____

_____

_____

_____

_____

_____

_____

_____

_____

_____

_____

EVENING ENCOURAGEMENT

WORDS OF LIFE TO MYSELF

A Servant's Heart

EXALT, ENCOURAGE, and UPLIFT.... that is
what God assigned my hands to do.
Little did I know that this assignment would
take me on some painful twists and turns.
Rejection, disappointments, pain, sickness, a weak
body, and poor decisions did not at all resemble the
assignment that I heard God speak over my life.
What I know He called me to was so far
from what I was experiencing.
How could the heartache that I felt translate
into the triumph that I anticipated?
There was a major discrepancy that my
mind could not rationalize.
I was walking through unfamiliar and uncomfortable
terrain that seemed so far from my assignment.
But then His Spirit revealed a glimmer of hope
that helped me reset and refocus.
He has implanted a servant's heart within me.
A servant's heart is sensitive, considerate,
available, and strong.
That only happens when the servant has tasted the
sweet, bitter, savory, and spicy things of life.
A servant's heart is secure and steady. It is not
unstable and selfish. It is devoted and consistent.
A servant's heart seeks opportunities to support.
It is grounded enough to put its own needs
aside, realizing that its satisfaction and needs
will be met and orchestrated in God's way.
So, in obedience, I trust God by embracing the servant's
heart that He has planted within me for His glory.
Lord, fulfill Your purpose in my life and allow me
to endure my challenges as a good soldier.
Regardless of what this life brings, Lord, make me
effective and ready for Your ministry of service.

SCRIPTURE REFERENCES

Philippians 4:13; Philippians 2:1-4;
Mark 10:45; Matthew 23:11-12

MORNING MEDITATION

EVENING ENCOURAGEMENT

WORDS OF LIFE TO MYSELF

He Will Fulfill His Purpose

Things are transitioning and shifting quickly.
It's almost frightening to see the
changes as I look in the mirror.
Although concerned, I am still peaceful and hopeful.
I'm not afraid of what I can't see because I
know there is purpose behind this pain.
I realize that my story will not finish being
written until God fulfills His purpose in me.
He has given me tasks and work that only fit my hands.
He has imparted ideas and gifts that only I can execute.
Although I am in a painful transition sometimes,
I take heart and cling to faith because I
completely understand this one thing….
God will not let me go and silence my song
until He has fulfilled His purpose in me.

SCRIPTURE REFERENCES

Psalm 138:8; Psalm 145:13; Psalm 139:14

MORNING MEDITATION

_____

_____

_____

_____

_____

_____

_____

_____

_____

_____

_____

_____

_____

_____

_____

EVENING ENCOURAGEMENT

WORDS OF LIFE TO MYSELF

Stillness

So many thoughts and concerns are flooding my mind.
So many responsibilities are before me.
I want to be a good steward of my time, so I plan
meticulously to ensure that nothing is missed.
Then, You touched my heart and brought
peace right into my situation.
You gave me STILLNESS, and it
brought such reassurance.
It feels different, but it's just what I needed.
Not only did the stillness come, but divine direction
and Your anointing were stillness' escorts.
With this combination, I'm at peace.
The challenges continue to come, but because of the
strategy of STILLNESS, I am not overwhelmed.
I'm prepared; I'm peaceful; I'm victorious!
My preparation came through STILLNESS,
and my heart is so glad!

SCRIPTURE REFERENCES

Psalm 46:10; Exodus 14:14; Isaiah 40:31

MORNING MEDITATION

EVENING ENCOURAGEMENT

WORDS OF LIFE TO MYSELF

Elevated

Excruciating pain, sleepless nights, fear,
and uncertainty about the future all gripped
my soul more than once or twice.
As a matter of fact, at times, it felt like
those thoughts would overtake me.
Yet I was blessed with the gift of time, and each
day was a new day with renewed hope.
My mind and spirit were fortified, despite
how my physical body felt.
Before I realized it, my inner being was elevated.
My thoughts and vision were different.
My spirit was more quiet and peaceful.
My interactions with others were different.
I found myself more intentional about my
schedule and more strategic about my choices.
When did this happen? As I was fighting for my life, had
there been a beautiful elevation that I didn't even realize?
My spirit, thoughts, and entire outlook had
been elevated right before my very eyes.
Somehow, I guess the tough days still brought
me to a beautiful place of elevation that
enhanced the very quality of my life.
Glory to God! I have been elevated!

SCRIPTURE REFERENCES

Romans 8:28; Philippians 4:13;
Psalm 20:4; Isaiah 40:31

MORNING MEDITATION

EVENING ENCOURAGEMENT

WORDS OF LIFE TO MYSELF

Not My Will

This season seems to be more than my
heart and my body could bear.
Mentally, there were too many times
of feeling overwhelmed.
There were too many times of physical aches and pains.
There seemed to be too many times of feeling
confused due to the impact of the medication.
There seemed to be too many times when
my body appeared to be shutting down.
There appeared to be too many times when the
prognosis was questionable and my future bleak.
But You spoke peace to my heart and into my situation.
And when You did, my body began to realign.
I was reassured by Your resounding
message that said, "Not my will."
Lord, I submit to the fact that it is not my will
but Your will that will be done in my life.

SCRIPTURE REFERENCES

Luke 22:42; Jeremiah 29:11;
1 Thessalonians 5:18; Proverbs 3:5-6

MORNING MEDITATION

_____

_____

_____

_____

_____

_____

_____

_____

_____

_____

_____

_____

_____

EVENING ENCOURAGEMENT

WORDS OF LIFE TO MYSELF

By Your Grace

This situation could have gone a different way.
This obstacle could have passed by me.
This pain could have been far from me,
never to have been experienced at all.
This diagnosis could have escaped
me, never afflicting my body.
Although I do not understand why I had to
endure this trauma, I know that it is by Your
grace that I can testify of Your goodness.
You have allowed me to come to this test so
that I can be a testimony of your grace.
It is by Your grace that I am still standing.
It is by Your grace that I am still rejoicing.
It is by Your grace that my hands go up
in victory when I think of You.
It is by Your grace that I am able to be here to say
just one more day that it is by Your grace that I live!

SCRIPTURE REFERENCES

2 Corinthians 12:8-9; 2 Peter 1:2;
Hebrews 4:16

MORNING MEDITATION

EVENING ENCOURAGEMENT

WORDS OF LIFE TO MYSELF

I Rose

Hands down, this has been the most difficult
journey and season of my life.
Words could not even explain to an observer
how hard this walk has been.
It has felt more like a dream as I reflect on
the many hurdles and obstacles.
Only my bed can attest to the groans and painful hours.
Only my pillow can speak of the tears that
soaked it night after night and day after day.
Only my God has witnessed the muted cries
for strength, grace, healing, and life.
Even now, the debilitating pain is a witness to
the length and intensity of this struggle.
Yet, I rose!
I rose each day, even if only briefly.
I rose in my emotions with the hope of better days.
I rose in my spirit as my faith increased with each
passing day and with each medical visit.
I rose in my vision, understanding that I must execute
every gift and plan that God has given me.
I rose in my purpose, realizing that I was created with a
specific assignment, and I will remain until it is fulfilled.
I rose in my love, knowing that the more I
spread it, the healthier I would become.
I rose in my attitude, resolving that I have every
reason to be positive and that I will pursue peace
every single day of my remaining existence.
I rose renewed and recreated for God's
purpose, and so have you.
So don't just rise; move forward!

SCRIPTURE REFERENCES

Psalm 73:26; Joshua 1:9; Isaiah 60:1;
Malachi 4:2; Deuteronomy 28:7

MORNING MEDITATION

EVENING ENCOURAGEMENT

WORDS OF LIFE TO MYSELF